DOMINOES

Pollyanna

LEVEL ONE   400 HEADWORDS

OXFORD
UNIVERSITY PRESS

Great Clarendon Street, Oxford OX2 6DP

Oxford University Press is a department of the University of Oxford.
It furthers the University's objective of excellence in research, scholarship,
and education by publishing worldwide in

Oxford New York

Auckland Cape Town Dar es Salaam Hong Kong Karachi
Kuala Lumpur Madrid Melbourne Mexico City Nairobi
New Delhi Shanghai Taipei Toronto

With offices in

Argentina Austria Brazil Chile Czech Republic France Greece
Guatemala Hungary Italy Japan Poland Portugal Singapore
South Korea Switzerland Thailand Turkey Ukraine Vietnam

OXFORD and OXFORD ENGLISH are registered trade marks of
Oxford University Press in the UK and in certain other countries

This edition © Oxford University Press 2010
The moral rights of the author have been asserted
Database right Oxford University Press (maker)
First published in Dominoes 2008

2022

19

ISBN: 978 0 19 424766 5 BOOK
ISBN: 978 0 19 463945 3 BOOK AND AUDIO PACK

No unauthorized photocopying

Printed in China

This book is printed on paper from certified and well-managed sources.

ACKNOWLEDGEMENTS

Cover: ITV/Carlton courtesy of Rex Features Still showing Georgina Terry, from *Pollyanna*,
2003, © ITV/Carlton

Illustrations by: Victor Tavares/Beehive Illustration

The publisher would like to thank the following for permission to reproduce photographs: Alamy Stock
Photo p44 (1873 illustration/Chronicle); Corbis pp25 (Boston and Maine railway station,
1900/Schenectady Museum; Hall of Electrical History Foundation), 38 (John Hopkins
hospital/Lake County Museum), 43 (women in car in 1900s); Getty Images p39 (Eleanor
H Porter/Culture Club); iStockphoto pp25 (rusty key/richcano); 31 (Chinese jewel case/
ChristianNasca); Kobal Collection pp44 (Heidi, 1937 film/20th Century Fox), 44 (The Secret
Garden/Am Zoetrope/Warner Bros/Close, Murray); Shutterstock pp13 (antique telephone/
Adrio Communications Ltd), 40 (ornamental picture frame/Marc Dietrich).

DOMINOES

Series Editors: Bill Bowler and Sue Parminter

Pollyanna

Eleanor H. Porter

Text adaptation by Bill Bowler

Illustrated by Victor Tavares

Eleanor Hodgman Porter was born in 1868 in New Hampshire, the United States. She was a singer when she was young, but later began writing. In 1892 she married John Lyman Porter, and moved to Massachusetts. Porter wrote short stories for magazines, lots of children's books, and a number of books for adults. The most famous of her children's books is *Pollyanna* (1913). It sold one million copies in its first year. Two years later, Porter wrote *Pollyanna Grows Up* – a book about Pollyanna when she is older. Porter died in Massachusetts in 1920.

OXFORD
UNIVERSITY PRESS

BEFORE READING

1 Look at the main characters in *Pollyanna*. What do you think of them? Use the words and phrases in the box to talk about them.

is poor
is rich
is friendly
is happy
lives alone
loves children
isn't friendly
doesn't have any parents
doesn't like children
has a big family

a Miss Polly Harrington . . .

b Nancy . . .

c Pollyanna . . .

d Jimmy Bean . . .

e Mr John Pendleton . . .

f Dr Chilton . . .

2 Complete these sentences with the character names. Talk about your ideas with a partner.

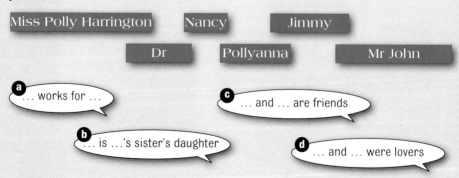

Miss Polly Harrington   Nancy   Jimmy

Dr   Pollyanna   Mr John

a . . . works for . . .

b . . . is . . .'s sister's daughter

c . . . and . . . are friends

d . . . and . . . were lovers

Chapter 1
Miss Polly

Miss Polly Harrington came quickly into her kitchen that June morning. 'Nancy, please stop your work for a minute and listen to me,' she said.

Nancy stopped at once. Miss Polly wasn't easy to please. Usually she wanted Nancy to work more quickly.

Nancy's father was dead, her mother was ill, and she had two younger sisters and a brother at home. So she came to work for Miss Harrington, one of the richest women in town. But Miss Polly was always angry when she did things badly, and never smiled when she did them right.

'Later today,' said Miss Polly, 'you can make the little back **attic** ready for a visitor. My **niece**, Miss Pollyanna Whittier, is coming to stay. She's eleven years old.'

'Is a little girl coming here? That's nice!' cried Nancy. She thought of her two happy little sisters at home.

'Nice?' said Miss Polly coldly. 'I don't know about that!'

Nancy's face was suddenly hot and red.

attic a little room at the top of a house

niece your sister's (or brother's) daughter

'But she's your sister's child, Miss. Of course you want her here.'

'Nancy, my **silly** sister **married** young, had children early, and couldn't **care for** them. I don't *want* to care for this child, but I must. Now don't forget that attic.' And with that, she left the kitchen.

＊ ＊

Back in her room, Miss Polly opened the letter from a far away town in the west and read it again:

> *Miss Harrington,*
>
> *I have **sad news** for you. Your sister's husband, John Whittier, died two weeks ago. He leaves a girl – eleven years old – behind him.*
>
> *John was the **Minister** in the **church** here, and wasn't very rich. His child has nobody to care for her now, only you – her family in the east. John spoke of this before he died.*
>
> *Can you take her? We can put Pollyanna on the train to come to you. When I get your answer – and please say 'yes' – I can write and tell you the day and time of the train.*
>
> *Jeremiah O. White*

silly not thinking well

marry to make someone your husband or wife

care for to do things for someone or something when they need it

sad not happy

news when someone tells you something that is new

minister a man who works for the church

church Christian people go here to pray

Miss Polly sat with the letter in her hand and thought of her sister Jennie, the girl's mother. When Jennie was twenty, a rich older man from the town wanted to marry her. But she wasn't interested in him or his money. She wanted to marry young John Whittier for love. Her parents weren't happy about it, but she didn't listen to them. She married, left home, and went west with her new husband.

Miss Polly remembered it well. She was only fifteen, the youngest, at the time. Her parents wanted nothing more to do with Jennie. Of course Jennie wrote for a time. Her letters told them about her different children, but they all died when they were very young. Only the last child lived. Jennie gave her the name Pollyanna after her two sisters, Polly and Anna. That was their last news from her. Some years later, a letter came for them from a small town in the

west. It was from John Whittier, and brought sad news: Jennie was dead.

Miss Polly thought about the past twenty-five years. She was forty years old. Her father, mother and sisters were all dead. The big family house, and all her father's money, were now in her name. Some people said to her, 'Why don't you live with a friend?' But she didn't want a friend in the house. She liked living quietly. And now...

Miss Polly stood up. She was happy, of course, to do the right thing and to take the girl into her home. But – *Pollyanna!* – what a silly name!

Later that morning Nancy made the back attic ready.

'Why is she putting the child here when she has lots of nicer rooms in the house to give her?' she thought.

That afternoon she went out into the garden to speak to Old Tom. He worked for Miss Polly there.

'Mr Tom, a little girl's coming to live here.' she said.

'Not with Miss Polly!' laughed Tom.

'Yes. She told me earlier today,' answered Nancy. 'It's her niece. She's eleven years old.'

'That's Miss Jennie's little girl then,' the old man said. 'And now she's coming to stay. That's wonderful.'

'She's going to sleep in the attic,' said Nancy. 'For me that's not right.'

Old Tom didn't look happy at this, but then he gave a big smile. 'Say, what's Miss Polly going to do with a child in the house?' he said.

'More important, what's a child going to do with Miss Polly in the house?' answered Nancy.

The old man laughed. 'You don't like Miss Polly,' he said.

'Nobody does,' answered Nancy.

'Ah, but you didn't know her when she was in love.'

'In love!' cried Nancy. 'Nobody loved her back, of course.'

'Oh, yes, they did,' said Old Tom. 'And the man's living here in the town today.'

'Who is he?'

'It's not right to tell you,' he said, and he looked up at the house. He was a true friend to the Harrington family. You could see it in his old blue eyes.

'So Miss Polly had a lover. I can't **believe** it,' said Nancy.

'Well, when she was younger, she was beautiful – and she can be again,' said old Tom.

'Beautiful! Miss Polly!'

'Yes. She needs to wear hats with flowers on them, to have her hair different, and to wear nice dresses again. Miss Polly's not old, Nancy.'

believe to think that something is true

'Well, she's never happy,' said Nancy. 'And one of these days I'm going to leave. Goodbye Nancy!'

'It's not easy for you, I know,' said Old Tom. 'But don't leave.' And with that, he went back to his work.

'Nancy!' called a cold voice from the house.

'Y-yes, Miss,' cried Nancy, and she ran in at once.

Some days later, Miss Polly told Nancy, 'My niece is arriving by train tomorrow at four. You can go with Timothy in the **buggy** and meet her. The letter says "**fair** hair, red dress, and a summer hat". You can find her with that, I'm **sure**.'

The next afternoon Nancy and Timothy, Old Tom's son, went to meet the train.

'Is she a good, quiet child, do you think?' asked Nancy.

'Who knows?' smiled Timothy. 'But a bad, noisy child isn't going to make things easy at the house for any of us, you can be sure of that!'

When the train arrived, a little girl with long fair hair, a red dress, and a summer hat got off. It was Pollyanna!

buggy an old kind of car that horses pull

fair yellow

sure when you feel that something is true

5

READING CHECK

Who are the sentences about?
Tick the columns.

	Miss Polly	Nancy	Pollyanna
a Her mother is ill.	☐	☑	☐
b Her mother was Miss Polly's sister.	☐	☐	☐
c She works for Miss Polly.	☐	☐	☐
d She lives alone in a big house.	☐	☐	☐
e She's got two younger sisters and a brother.	☐	☐	☐
f She's rich.	☐	☐	☐
g Her mother and father both died young.	☐	☐	☐
h Her family doesn't have much money.	☐	☐	☐
i She has nowhere to live.	☐	☐	☐
j She isn't very friendly.	☐	☐	☐

WORD WORK

1 Match the words in the box with the underlined words in the conversation.

believe	care for	~~news~~	niece	silly	sure

A: Did you hear the <u>new story</u> about
   Miranda? **a** .... *news* .....

B: About my <u>brother's daughter</u>?
   b ....

A: That's right. She left school
   to <u>do things to help</u> animals.
   c ....

B: I can't <u>truly think</u> it . Did she tell
   you that? **d** ....

A: <u>That's right</u>. **e** ....

B: But that's <u>not thinking well</u>. She was a
   good student! **f** ....

2 Look at the pictures and complete the sentences with new words from Chapter 1.

a Pollyanna's room is in the ....attic..... of Miss Polly's house.

b My grandmother is never happy and always has a very .... face.

c Pollyanna's father was a .... in a town in the west.

d Most people in our village go to .... every Sunday.

e Timothy and Nancy went in the .... to the station.

f 'Please .... me, Daisy,' said James. 'I want you for my wife.'

g Pollyanna's hair is long and .... in colour.

GUESS WHAT

What happens to Pollyanna in Chapter Two? Tick three things.

a ☐ She meets Miss Polly.

b ☐ Miss Polly is very nice to her.

c ☐ She's late for supper, and Miss Polly is angry with her.

d ☐ She cries about everything in Miss Polly's house.

e ☐ Miss Polly gives her some new clothes.

Chapter 2
The glad game

Soon Pollyanna was in the buggy between Timothy and Nancy, and they were on the road to Miss Polly's house.

'I didn't have a black dress to wear,' said Pollyanna. 'But it's easier to be **glad** in red than black, I **guess**.'

'"Glad"!' cried Nancy.

'Yes. Because now Father's with Mother and my dead brothers and sisters. Father said that before he died. And of course I'm glad, too, because I have you, **Aunt** Polly.'

'Me? But I'm Nancy. I work for Miss Polly.'

'Oh, I see,' answered Pollyanna. 'So she didn't come to meet me. Well . . . I'm glad about that. Because now I have you, and I'm going to meet her soon, too.'

glad happy

guess to think

aunt your mother's (or father's) sister

Miss Polly was in the front room when they arrived. 'Hello, Pollyanna,' she said without a smile.

Pollyanna ran and took the older woman in her arms. 'I'm very glad to meet you, Aunt Polly. Now, about my red dress: Father said–'

'Let's not talk about your father, child. Your bag–'

'There isn't much in it. Only Father's books, and–'

'Pollyanna, I don't want to hear about your father. Do you understand?'

'Yes, Aunt Polly,' said the girl sadly.

'Your bag's in your room,' Aunt Polly finished. 'Timothy took it up. So come with me.'

Pollyanna went upstairs after her aunt. There were lots of beautiful pictures to left and right, wonderful rooms, and a nice green **carpet** under her feet. But when they went into her room, it had no pictures or carpet in it – only a bed, a chair, a window, a table, and a **closet**.

'Here we are,' said Miss Polly. 'Nancy can help you put your things away. **Supper**'s at six o'clock.' And with that, she went downstairs.

When Nancy came up, she found Pollyanna with her hands over her face. Sadly the girl opened her bag, and Nancy took some old dresses and books from it, and put them away.

At the same time, Pollyanna looked through the window. 'Oh Nancy, I don't need pictures when I can see houses, trees, and the river through this,' she said.

Just then, they heard a **bell** downstairs.

'I must go now,' said Nancy, and she went down to help with the supper.

Pollyanna soon felt hot in her room, and she opened the window. Then, with a laugh, she **climbed** out through the window, down the tree in front of it, and into the garden. From there she ran to a little hill not far away. Old Tom was in the garden and he saw her go. Soon she was up the hill, and she didn't hear the supper bell at six o'clock.

carpet a piece of thick material that you put on the floor

closet a big piece of furniture where you put things to wear

supper when you eat in the evening

bell a metal thing that makes a noise when you move it

climb to go up, down, or through something using your hands and feet

'My niece is late,' said Miss Polly to Nancy at the supper table. 'She can have bread and milk in the kitchen.'

After supper Nancy went upstairs, but Pollyanna wasn't in her room. So Nancy went out into the garden.

'Pollyanna's up the hill over there,' said Old Tom.

Nancy went at once and brought the girl in.

'How did you get out there?' Nancy asked.

Pollyanna told her.

'Well, you were late for supper. So you must have bread and milk with me in the kitchen tonight, your aunt says.'

'Oh, I'm glad,' smiled Pollyanna. 'I like bread and milk. And I'd like to have supper with you, too.'

'How can you be glad about everything?'

'Well, It's the "glad **game**" you know. My father taught it to me. You must always find the good in everything and be glad about it. It isn't always easy.'

Before bed, Miss Polly spoke to her niece.

'I'm sorry about supper tonight, Pollyanna, but you must learn to be on time.'

'Oh, don't feel bad, Aunt Polly,' said Pollyanna, 'I was glad to have bread and milk in the kitchen with Nancy.'

The next afternoon, Miss Polly took Pollyanna into town. 'We must get you some new **clothes**,' she said.

'New clothes!' cried Pollyanna. 'You're very good to me.'

'I don't know about "good",' answered Miss Polly. 'With you in old clothes people are going to think badly of me. I don't want that!'

'Of course not,' said Pollyanna. 'And you *are* good, Aunt Polly. But you don't feel glad about it. Why not? I'm always glad when I do something good.'

game something that you play; tennis and football are games

clothes people wear these

'Be quiet, child,' said Miss Polly. 'Or we're going home this minute.'

Pollyanna stopped talking at once.

That evening it was very hot again in Pollyanna's room, and she couldn't sleep. So she got out of bed and went to the back attic room. She opened the window there, and climbed out onto the **roof** of Miss Polly's room.

'I can sleep here,' she thought.

But Miss Polly heard noises in the night, and called Timothy on the telephone.

'Come quickly. There's someone on my roof,' she cried.

When Timothy came, he found Pollyanna out on the roof, and took her in.

'What were you doing on my roof, girl?' asked Miss Polly angrily.

'Oh, Aunt Polly, I wanted to sleep out under the night sky–' began Pollyanna.

'Well, now you must sleep in bed with me tonight, Pollyanna. Because I don't want this to happen again.'

'Oh, thank you,' cried Pollyanna. 'What a wonderful thing to sleep in my aunt's bed!'

Miss Polly couldn't speak. Why, when she wanted to **punish** her niece, was the girl always glad?

roof the thing on top of a building that stops the rain coming in

punish to do something bad to someone after they do something bad

READING CHECK

1 Choose the true answers about Pollyanna's 'glad game'.

a Who taught it to her?

   1 ☑ Her father.

   2 ☐ Her mother.

   3 ☐ A church minister.

b Is it a game only for children?

   1 ☐ Yes, it is.

   2 ☐ No, it's for everybody.

   3 ☐ No, it's for men and women.

c When does she play it?

   1 ☐ When bad things happen.

   2 ☐ When good things happen.

   3 ☐ When she's happy.

d How does she play it?

   1 ☐ She cries a lot about everything.

   2 ☐ She does bad things and feels glad.

   3 ☐ She finds something to be happy about

2 Pollyanna plays the 'glad game' about different things in Chapter Two. Tick the things.

a ☐ riding in the buggy

b ☑ her red dress

c ☐ aunt Polly not meeting her at the station

d ☐ her father

e ☐ her old dresses and books

f ☐ her room in the attic with no pictures

g ☐ Old Tom in the garden

h ☐ having bread and milk for supper

i ☐ her hot room

j ☐ sleeping with her aunt

WORD WORK

1 Circle the words from Chapter Two in the telephone.

2 Complete the sentences with the words from 1.

a Tom was bad today. You must ....punish.... him.

b That's the ....! Get the door Amy!

c There isn't a .... on the attic floor.

d Can you .... the tree and get my cat?

e I put your new dress in the ....

f We're going out for .... tonight.

g 'She doesn't like children much, I ....'

h New York's cold now. Bring warm ....

i What .... are those children playing?

j .... Peggy is my father's sister.

k You came to see me today. I'm very .... about that.

l Pollyanna slept on the .... because it was hot in her room.

a punish ge carpet rn guess on clothes floa aunt rac loset be supper li gla dee bel l stcl imbel ga mel e roof

3 Write the extra letters in the telephone in order to find the names of Nancy's brother: (_ _ _ _ _ _ _), and two sisters:(_ _ _ _ _ _ _ _ _ _, _ _ _ _ _ _).

GUESS WHAT

1 Pollyanna meets these three people in Chapter 3. Match the names with the sentences.

a .... has no mother or father, and wants a family.

b .... is ill all the time, and never gets out of bed.

c .... is very rich, but has nobody to talk to.

Mrs Snow

John Pendleton

Jimmy Bean

2 How does Pollyanna help all three of them, do you think?

Chapter 3

New friends

The weeks went by, and Pollyanna felt happy in her new home – but it wasn't easy to talk to Miss Polly. Nancy was Pollyanna's only friend, and she always had work to do. So Pollyanna wanted to go out and meet people.

Mrs Snow lived not far away. She was a very **sick** woman, and never left her bed. Miss Polly usually sent Nancy to her house on Thursday afternoons with something for her to eat – **chicken**, **soup**, or **jelly**.

'Can *I* go today?' Pollyanna asked Nancy one Thursday.

'Mrs Snow's never happy,' said Nancy. 'When she gets chicken, she wants soup. When it's soup, she wants jelly. You don't want to go.'

'Yes, I do.'

So Pollyanna went to Mrs Snow's house that afternoon. Miss Snow, a tired young woman, took the girl to her mother – and left her there in the dark room.

'Here's some jelly from Aunt Polly,' said Pollyanna.

'I wanted soup today,' said Mrs Snow from the bed.

'That's **strange**!' cried Pollyanna. 'Usually you want chicken when you get jelly, and soup when it's chicken.

sick ill

chicken meat from a bird that has eggs which people eat

soup a food that you make by cooking vegetables or meat in water

jelly a soft, tasty food that you can see through which you can make with meat or fruit

strange not usual

Nancy told me.'

Mrs Snow sat up. 'What a thing to say!' she cried. 'Who are you?'

'I'm Miss Polly's niece. I live with her now, and I'm here with your jelly!'

'I'm not hungry. I didn't sleep at all last night,' said Mrs Snow.

'That's wonderful!' said Pollyanna. 'We lose lots of time when we sleep. I'd like not to sleep at night, too.'

'What's that?! Open the **curtains**. I want to see you,' said Mrs Snow.

So Pollyanna opened the curtains.

'You're beautiful!' cried Pollyanna, when she saw Mrs Snow in the sun. 'I love your dark eyes and hair.'

That afternoon Pollyanna did Mrs Snow's hair, and put a **pink** flower in it.

Miss Snow had a **surprise** when she came in after Pollyanna left. 'Mother, the curtains!' she cried.

'I wanted them open,' said Mrs Snow. 'And why do people bring me only things to eat. I'd like something nice to wear sometimes, too!'

In September, after a long summer, Pollyanna started school. On her first morning, she met a man in the street. He wore a tall black hat and a long black coat, and he didn't smile.

curtains people close these in front of windows to stop the sun from coming into dark rooms

pink a colour between red and white

surprise when you feel that something very new is suddenly happening

'It's a nice day,' said Pollyanna.

'Are you talking to me?' he said angrily. He didn't stop.

The next day when Pollyanna saw him, he had an **umbrella**. 'I don't like it when it rains,' she said. 'But it doesn't rain every day. I'm glad about that.'

The man said nothing. 'Did he hear me?' she thought.

The day after, when they next met, the sun was in the sky. Pollyanna said, 'It's a nicer day than yesterday.'

'Who are you?' said the man angrily. 'And why do you always tell me about the weather? I have more important things to think about!'

'I'm telling you because you don't have time to look at the sky. I'm Pollyanna Whittier. Who are you?'

'Why of all the – !' began the man. Then he walked away.

The next time Pollyanna met him, he said, 'Good afternoon. And before you speak, can I say something? It's a beautiful day, and I know it.'

'Yes. I saw it in your smile before you spoke,' said Pollyanna.

'Did you?' answered the man.

━ ━

Nancy had a surprise when she went for a walk with Pollyanna, and the man said 'good afternoon' to them.

'He spoke to you!' Nancy cried.

'Yes, he always does – now,' answered Pollyanna.

'But that's John Pendleton. He lives **alone** in a house on Pendleton Hill. He never speaks to people. My friend Sally works at the hotel in town, and he never talks when he eats there. He never eats expensively, of course.'

'It isn't easy without money,' said Pollyanna.

'He's the richest man in town,' answered Nancy. 'But he

umbrella a thing that you hold over your head to keep you dry when it rains

alone with nobody

doesn't like giving his money away. He's strange.'

'Maybe he's strange when you don't know him,' said Pollyanna. 'But I like him.'

At about that time, Pollyanna found a little cat in the street and took it home. After that she found a little dog and took that home, too. Miss Polly didn't like animals, but it wasn't easy to say 'no' to Pollyanna. So Fluffy the cat, and Buffy the dog stayed.

October came, and one day Pollyanna met a boy in the street near her house. He was thin and in old clothes. 'Who are you?' asked Pollyanna, 'And what are you doing here?'

'I'm Jimmy Bean. I left the **Orphans'** Home this morning. I want to find a **real** home, with real **folks**, see.'

It wasn't easy to lose your mother and father, Pollyanna knew. So she took Jimmy home.

'Aunt Polly, can Jimmy Bean live with us?' she asked.

But Aunt Polly said 'No!' and Jimmy left the house sadly. Pollyanna ran after him.

'Don't worry. I'm going to find you a real home,' she told him in the street. 'Maybe the church can help. Let's see.'

So Jimmy went back to the Orphans' Home that night, and Aunt Polly felt bad. The next day she told Nancy, 'Please move Pollyanna's things down from the attic into the bedroom under it.'

orphan a child without a mother or father or family to care for it

real true

folks family; people

17

READING CHECK

Mark these sentences true or false.

		True	False
a	Aunt Polly talks a lot with Pollyanna.	☐	☑
b	Pollyanna visits Mrs Snow because she's ill.	☐	☐
c	Mrs Snow never gets out of bed.	☐	☐
d	Mrs Snow is happy to see Pollyanna at first.	☐	☐
e	Pollyanna meets John Pendleton at school.	☐	☐
f	John Pendleton doesn't talk to Pollyanna at first.	☐	☐
g	Nancy is sad when John Pendleton speaks to Pollyanna.	☐	☐
h	Pollyanna meets Jimmy Bean in the street.	☐	☐
i	Jimmy Bean wants to find a new home.	☐	☐
j	Aunt Polly gives Pollyanna a new bedroom.	☐	☐

WORD WORK

1 Use the letters to complete the labels for the pictures.

a j e l l y   **b** u _ _ _ e _ _ a

c _ o u _   **d** _ u _ _ a i _ _   **e** _ _ i _ _ e _   **f** _ i _ _

2 Unjumble the letters in the jellies to complete the sentences.

a My aunt doesn't live with anyone.
She lives .... *alone* ......

b Jimmy Bean's parents are dead.
He doesn't have any ....

c I didn't leave my bed at the weekend because I
had a bad head and felt very ....

d Pollyanna's parents are dead.
She's an ....

e We know lots of people, but we have only
one or two .... friends.

f Pollyanna's old clothes aren't very usual.
They're ....

g She had a birthday .... When she came home
all her friends were there and she knew nothing about it.

GUESS WHAT

**The next chapter is called *Things go wrong*. What problems are you
going to read about? Match the people with the problems.**

Aunt Polly	Mr Pendleton	Jimmy Bean	Pollyanna

a ▨▨▨▨ has a bad accident.
b One of ▨▨▨▨ 's friends is very sick and dies.
c Pollyanna can't find a home for ▨▨▨▨ .
d Aunt Polly gets angry with ▨▨▨▨ .

Chapter 4
Things go wrong

When Nancy told Pollyanna about her new bedroom, she ran at once to her aunt.

'It's beautiful,' she cried, 'with its pictures, carpet, and curtains. Thank you, Aunt Polly. I'm really glad.'

'Pollyanna, please stop being "glad" about everything. I'm tired of it. You always say it. Why?'

'It comes from our game. Father—' Pollyanna began, and then stopped. Aunt Polly didn't like to hear about her father. So she said nothing more about it.

After dinner that day Miss Polly phoned the Minister's wife. 'I'm sorry but I can't come to the **charity meeting** at the church this afternoon. I have a bad head.'

When Miss Polly went to her room, Pollyanna went out.

'Good afternoon **ladies**, I'm Pollyanna Whittier,' she said when she went into the church meeting.

'Did your aunt **send** you?' asked the Minister's wife.

'No. It was my **idea**,' said Pollyanna. 'I want to help Jimmy Bean — a boy from the Orphans' Home. He's ten years old, and he wants real folks and a real home. Can one of you ladies take him into your house?'

The ladies talked a lot. But not one wanted to take Jimmy. In the end Pollyanna left the church sadly.

She didn't go home, but walked far into Pendleton **woods**. There she found Mr John Pendleton on the **ground**.

'What's the matter?' she asked.

'I **fell** from those **rocks** up there, and broke my leg,' he said. 'I can't move.'

Then he took a **key** from his coat and gave it to her.

charity helping poor people

meeting when a number of people come to talk about something important

lady a woman from a good family

send (*past* **sent**) to make someone go somewhere; to give something to someone to take somewhere for you

idea something that you think

woods a place where lots of trees grow together

ground we walk on this

fall (*past* **fell**) to go down suddenly

rock a big stone

key you can close or open a door with this

'Here's the key to my house. It's not far past those trees. Go there, open the front door, and go in. By the door there's a telephone, and a telephone book. Find Dr Thomas Chilton's number and phone him. Tell him about my accident near Pendleton Hill Rocks. Then wait there for him to arrive, and bring him here.'

Pollyanna went off with the key and was soon back.

'Did you get in?' Mr Pendleton asked.

'Yes, and I phoned, and Dr Chilton's coming. But I wanted to stay with you.'

When Dr Chilton came, he smiled at Pollyanna. 'Thank you, young lady, for your help.'

Then he looked carefully at Mr Pendleton's leg.

———

That evening Pollyanna arrived late for supper. Nancy met her at the door. 'Your aunt isn't here. She went to Boston suddenly to visit a sick friend. And I'm glad.'

'Nancy!' cried Pollyanna.

'It's OK. I'm playing the glad game,' laughed Nancy.

Then Pollyanna told Nancy about John Pendleton's accident, and she listened with an open mouth.

———

The next day Pollyanna told Jimmy Bean about the ladies' charity meeting. 'I'm sorry,' she said. 'They were more interested in their charity work in India than in you. It's because India's far away, I guess.'

Then she had an idea. 'I know! I can write to the ladies from my father's old church out west. Maybe they'd like to help you because you're far away.'

'OK,' said Jimmy, and he went back to the Orphans' Home again that night.

Three days later, after her friend in Boston died, Miss Polly came back home.

'Can I take Mrs Snow's jelly to someone different today?' asked Pollyanna that Thursday. 'He broke his leg and he needs the jelly more than Mrs Snow at the moment.'

And Pollyanna told her aunt all about John Pendleton's accident.

'John Pendleton!' cried Miss Polly. 'Do you know him?'

'Yes,' said Pollyanna. 'So can I take him the jelly?'

'Very well,' said her aunt, 'But I didn't send you. You must be careful not to say that.'

Pollyanna found Dr Chilton at John Pendleton's house.

'Come in,' the doctor said, and Pollyanna went into Mr Pendleton's room.

'Why are you here?' cried the man in bed angrily.

'I brought you some jelly,' said Pollyanna. 'Nancy made it. She works for Aunt Polly.'

'Aunt Polly?'

'Miss Polly Harrington. I live with her.'

'With – *her*?' he said. His face was suddenly white.

'Yes. My mother was her sister. When Father died, they sent me to her.'

'Did Miss Polly send that jelly for me?'

'Oh, no! I must be careful not to say that. She told me.'

'I see,' said Mr Pendleton, and he looked at Pollyanna very strangely.

Dr Chilton took her home in his buggy soon after that.

A week after Pollyanna's visit to Mr Pendleton's house, Miss Polly went to a ladies' charity meeting at the church.

When she came home, her face was pink and her hair was dark from the rain.

'Why did you go to them about that orphan boy, Pollyanna?' she asked her niece. 'It was very bad of you.'

Pollyanna didn't listen. 'Your hair's beautiful today, Aunt Polly!' she said.

She took her aunt up to her room, did her hair, and put a red flower in it. And Miss Polly couldn't stop her, couldn't punish her. Then – suddenly – through the window they saw Dr Chilton's buggy in the street, with the doctor in it.

Pollyanna opened the window and called out to him. 'Dr Chilton, did you want me? I'm up here!'

Miss Polly ran from the window at once.

'What's the matter?' Pollyanna called after her.

'Why did you do that? It's not right for folks to see me with a silly flower in my hair,' cried her aunt.

READING CHECK

Correct the mistakes in the sentences.

a Pollyanna is very ~~sad~~ *happy* about her new bedroom.

b Aunt Polly doesn't go out because she feels tired.

c Pollyanna talks to some women at the church about Aunt Polly.

d Mr Pendleton breaks his arm in an accident.

e Pollyanna phones the doctor from Aunt Polly's house.

f Aunt Polly goes to Boston to visit her sister.

g Pollyanna takes Mr Pendleton some soup.

h Mr Pendleton is happy because Pollyanna is Miss Polly's niece.

i Dr Chilton sees Pollyanna with a flower in her hair.

WORD WORK

1 Write out the sentences using words from Chapter 4.

a He down and broke his leg. *He fell down and broke his leg.*

b Shall we go for a walk in the ? ....

c Don't put your books down on the  ! ....

d There are some big in the road. ....

e The is in the door. ....

2 Use the words in the key to complete the gaps in Pollyanna's letter.

charity

idea

send

ladies

meeting

Dear Friends,

I'm writing to you with an (a) ...idea... .
I want to help Jimmy Bean – a boy from the
Orphans' Home here. He wants real folks and a
real home. I went to a church (b) .... here,
but no one wants Jimmy in their home. The church
(c) .... here are interested in (d) ....
work in India, not in this town.

Maybe I can (e) .... Jimmy to live with
one of you folks because you live far away. What do
you think? Please write soon.

Pollyanna

GUESS WHAT

What do you think happens in the next chapter?   **Yes**   **No**

a A family from out west wants Jimmy Bean to live with them.   ☐   ☐

b Mr Pendleton wants Pollyanna to live with him.   ☐   ☐

c Nancy tells Pollyanna, 'Mr Pendleton and Aunt Polly were lovers.'   ☐   ☐

d Mr Pendleton tells Pollyanna, 'I loved your mother.'   ☐   ☐

e Dr Chilton tells Pollyanna that he loves Aunt Polly.   ☐   ☐

f Pollyanna goes to live with Mr Pendleton.   ☐   ☐

Chapter 5
Someone very important

Pollyanna left her aunt upstairs and ran out to Dr Chilton. 'What is it?' she asked.

'Mr Pendleton wants you. So – after the rain stopped – I drove over here. Can you come?'

'I must ask my aunt.'

She came back nearly at once.

'Well?' asked the doctor.

'I can go,' Pollyanna answered. 'But Aunt Polly spoke very strangely to me. She said, "Yes, go. Why didn't you leave before?".'

'Was your aunt upstairs at the window with you when I arrived?' asked the doctor.

'Yes. Did you see her? She was beautiful, I thought. What did you think?'

The doctor looked at Pollyanna – smiled sadly – and said, 'Yes, for me she was – beautiful, too.'

'Oh, I must tell her!'

'Pollyanna, please don't.'

'Why not? It's a nice thing to say.'

'But maybe Miss Polly doesn't want to hear it from me.'

'Maybe you're right. Dr Warren's her doctor, after all – and she ran from the window when she saw you here.'

And with that, they went to Mr Pendleton's house.

━ ━

Mr Pendleton was very happy to see her. 'Do you have more jelly for me, <u>not</u> from Aunt Polly?' he laughed.

Pollyanna's face was suddenly red.

'Did I say something wrong on my last visit?' she asked.

'No,' he answered.

He had a box of beautiful old things from China and India by his bed that day. They opened it, and took them out, and Pollyanna played with them. And he and Pollyanna talked. They spoke of Nancy, Aunt Polly, and Pollyanna's home with her father and mother out west.

When it was time for her to go, John Pendleton said quietly, 'Pollyanna, when I learnt about your folks last time, I didn't want to see you again. You **reminded** me of someone once very important for me, from years ago, and I felt sad. I wanted to forget you. But I can't do without you – I know that now. So please come and see me often.'

'Of course,' said Pollyanna.

After supper Pollyanna told Nancy about her visit.

'Lots of people don't like him. But he's very nice to me,' she said. 'And it isn't always easy. When I took him the jelly on my last visit, and

remind to make somebody remember something

he heard about my folks, he didn't want to see me again.'

'Why's that?' asked Nancy.

And Pollyanna told Nancy about the 'someone very important' for Mr Pendleton from years ago.

'That's it!' cried Nancy. 'Now I understand.'

'What?' asked Pollyanna.

'Mr John Pendleton and Miss Polly Harrington were lovers all those years ago!' cried Nancy, and she told Pollyanna about Old Tom's story.

'But Mr Pendleton doesn't like Aunt Polly,' said Pollyanna, 'and she didn't want to send him the jelly.'

'That's because they **quarrelled**,' said Nancy.

On Pollyanna's next visit to John Pendleton's house, before she left, he again had a quiet talk with her.

'I feel very alone in this big old house, Pollyanna. I need a woman's hand and **heart**, or a child's face, near me to feel at home here. Would you like to come and live with me? Maybe I can **adopt** you.'

'With Aunt Polly?' asked Pollyanna. 'Can she come, too?'

'Aunt Polly?!'

'Yes, because you loved her all those years ago.'

'Well, no – not with Aunt Polly,' he answered with a red face. 'And please don't tell people about my **plan** for now. It's a **secret**. Do you understand?'

The next time Dr Chilton took Pollyanna to Mr Pendleton's house, she said, 'I'm going to tell you something, Dr Chilton. It's a secret between Mr Pendleton and me. But I can tell you, I think. It's only a secret from her.'

'Her?' asked Dr Chilton.

'Aunt Polly,' said Pollyanna, and she told the doctor all

quarrel to talk angrily with someone

heart the centre of feeling in somebody

adopt to take a child into your home to be your son or daughter

plan when you get something ready to do later

secret something that you don't tell to everybody

about the old love between Mr Pendleton and her aunt, and about Mr Pendleton's plans to adopt her.

'Right. I didn't know about that,' said the doctor, and he was quiet for a long time.

'Maybe Mr Pendleton wants to tell me more about it today,' said Pollyanna, when they arrived.

'Maybe,' said Doctor Chilton, and he smiled strangely and drove off in his buggy back to town.

On that visit Mr Pendleton **explained** everything.

'I didn't love *Aunt Polly* all those years ago,' he told Pollyanna. 'I was in love with *your mother*, before she married your father. But she didn't love me back.'

'Oh, I see!' cried Pollyanna.

'When I met you, you reminded me of her. At first I didn't want to see you again. But now I want to adopt you.'

'And what about Aunt Polly?'

'No, I want only you. So can you ask her about it?'

'All right.'

After her visit, Pollyanna walked back home. It began to rain after she left Pendleton woods, but soon she met Nancy in the street with an umbrella.

'Miss Polly sent me to find you with this,' said Nancy. 'She was really **worried** about you.'

'Was she?' asked Pollyanna. She couldn't leave her aunt and live with Mr Pendleton now, she knew that. Aunt Polly was worried about her, and needed her. But Mr Pendleton really needed a child near him, too, to make his big old house into a home. What could Pollyanna do to make the two of them happy?

Suddenly she smiled. She had the answer.

explain to talk to someone and make them understand something

worried not happy about something and thinking a lot about it

READING CHECK

Who said what? Match the speech bubbles with the speakers.

a Yes, for me she was – beautiful, too.

c It's a secret between Mr Pendleton and me.

b When he heard about my folks, he didn't want to see me again.

d Would you like to come and live with me?

f But she didn't love me back.

e She was really worried about you.

1 Nancy is speaking to Pollyanna about Miss Polly. — `e`

2 Mr Pendleton is speaking to Pollyanna about the future. ☐

3 Pollyanna is speaking to Nancy about Mr Pendleton. ☐

4 Dr Chilton is speaking to Pollyanna about Miss Polly. ☐

5 Mr Pendleton is speaking to Pollyanna about her mother. ☐

6 Pollyanna is speaking to Dr Chilton about Mr Pendleton and Aunt Polly. ☐

WORD WORK

Use new words from Chapter 5 to do the crossword on page 31.

→ Across

2 Please don't tell anyone. It's a ......*secret*......

6 We can't have children so we're going to .... a little boy.

7 What's your .... for this evening?

8 I .... with my mother because I got home late.

↓ Down

1 .... me to phone the doctor when we get home.

3 Can you .... how this radio works?

4 There is love in my .... for you.

5 I'm .... because I've got an English test tomorrow.

Crossword puzzle:
2 (across): s e c r e t

GUESS WHAT

What do you think happens at the end of Pollyanna?

a Pollyanna ☐   Aunt Polly ☐
. . . has a bad accident.

b Pollyanna ☐   Jimmy Bean ☐
. . . goes to live with Mr Pendleton.

c Jimmy Bean ☐   Mr Pendleton ☐
. . . speaks to Aunt Polly about Dr Chilton.

d Dr Chilton ☐   Mr Pendleton ☐
. . . marries Aunt Polly.

Chapter 6
The gladdest things

poor without money; something you say when you feel sorry for someone

invitation when someone asks you to go somewhere

medicine something that you eat or drink to help you get better when you are ill

On Pollyanna's next visit to John Pendleton's house, he asked, 'Did you speak to your aunt? Can you live here?'

'No, I can't.'

'Did she say "no"?'

'I didn't ask her – but she needs me. And I have a different child for you to adopt – to make your house into a home. I'm really glad for him.'

'For who?'

'Jimmy Bean!' cried Pollyanna, and she explained about the **poor** orphan. 'I had a letter from my church ladies out west last week,' she finished, 'and nobody wanted him there. He was sad about that.'

Pollyanna left with an **invitation** for Jimmy and her to visit Mr Pendleton next Saturday.

One Thursday afternoon, Mrs Snow sent Pollyanna to Dr Chilton's house for some **medicine**.

'I never saw your home before,' she said.

'They're only rooms,' he answered. 'Not really a home.'

32

'Do you need the hand and heart of a woman or the face of a child, too? Mr Pendleton wanted those,' said Pollyanna. 'Oh, and you remember when I told you about him and Aunt Polly: did you tell any folks that story?'

'No.'

'Good. Because Mr Pendleton explained everything to me later. He loved my mother, not Aunt Polly. But now he's going to adopt Jimmy Bean. So maybe you can get the hand and heart of a woman, or the face of a child, to make *your* rooms into a home, Dr Chilton.'

'Some women don't give hand and heart very easily,' he answered quickly, and stood up. 'Here's that medicine for Mrs Snow,' he said.

→ ←

All of this of course was before the accident, and that changed everything. How did it happen? On the last day of October, Pollyanna left school. She didn't look to left and right when she walked across the road. Suddenly a car hit her, and she fell to the ground **unconscious**. By five o'clock she was back at home, but when would she open her eyes? Nancy sat by her bed, and Miss Polly telephoned her doctor at once.

When Dr Warren came, he looked at Pollyanna carefully. 'Well, she didn't break an arm or a leg, but she hit her head badly,' he told Miss Polly. 'And I'm worried.'

Next morning Pollyanna opened her eyes. 'Where am I? What happened? Why can't I move my legs?' she cried.

Miss Polly explained about the accident. 'And now you must sleep,' she said.

So Pollyanna slept for days. And many people from the town came and left flowers for her.

unconscious sleeping because you are ill or something hit you

When John Pendleton arrived, soon after Pollyanna's accident, Nancy ran to tell Old Tom.

'Mr Pendleton's here.'

'You don't say!' answered the old man.

'Was he really Miss Polly's lover from long ago?' asked Nancy. 'I believed that once, but now I'm not sure.'

'Don't be silly. He loved Miss Jennie. But she loved that young Minister. When they married and left, Miss Polly felt sorry for John Pendleton and was nice to him. Maybe he understood something different, but for her they were only good friends. Then – in the town – people began to talk of love between them. After that, Miss Polly and John Pendleton quarrelled and he stopped coming here.'

In the front room, Mr Pendleton asked, 'How is Pollyanna?'

'I don't know,' said Miss Polly coldly. 'She can't move her legs, but she talks about when you broke your leg and were in bed for only weeks. She's "glad" because that's different from poor Mrs Snow – in bed for years. It's very sad. She doesn't understand.'

'I wanted Pollyanna to live with me, you know,' he said.

'With you?' said Miss Polly.

'Yes, but she wanted to stay here, because you needed her, she said.'

Suddenly **tears** came to Miss Polly's eyes.

tear the water that comes from your eye when you cry

specialist a very important doctor who knows a lot about one part of the body

push to move something with your body

After some weeks Dr Warren called a **specialist** from New York. Dr Mead came and looked at Pollyanna. When he left, he spoke quietly to Miss Polly by Pollyanna's door.

Fluffy the cat was in Pollyanna's room at the time, and she wanted to go out. Just then, she **pushed** the door open. So Pollyanna heard everything.

'Well, she's never going to walk again,' said Dr Mead.

Poor Pollyanna! When she was well, she taught the 'glad game' to Mr Pendleton, Mrs Snow, Nancy and lots of people in town. But now she could never leave her bed, it wasn't easy for her to find a thing to be glad about.

Mr John Pendleton called on Aunt Polly again when he heard the news.

'Please tell Pollyanna something from me,' he said before he left. 'Jimmy Bean came to see me, and he's going to be my little boy. I'm going to adopt him. Tell her that. Maybe she can feel glad about it.'

'Yes, Mr Pendleton,' said Miss Polly in surprise.

Pollyanna was of course very glad to hear the news.

Back home, Mr Pendleton and his friend Dr Chilton sat in the front room and talked. 'You remember your friend at the hospital, Tom?'

'Who? The specialist.'

'Yes. He helps lots of people to walk after accidents. Take Pollyanna to him. Maybe he can help her, too.'

'I can't, John. I must have a look at her before I can call my friend. But Dr Warren is Miss Polly's doctor. I can't visit without an invitation from him. And after Miss Polly and I quarrelled fifteen years ago – when folks in town began to call the two of you lovers – she's never going to ask me. You know that. I'm never going to visit her house again without an invitation from her. And she's never going to change her heart, and **forgive** me.'

'Please, Tom. Forget all that. Think of the girl.'

'I'm sorry, John. But without an invitation from Miss Polly, I can't visit Pollyanna.'

Now all this time the window in the room was open. And near the window – because it was Saturday morning – Jimmy Bean was at work in the garden. He heard everything, and went at once to speak to Miss Polly.

That afternoon an invitation came for Dr Chilton to visit Pollyanna.

'Did you ask for me?' Dr Chilton asked Miss Polly when he arrived.

'I-I did,' said Miss Polly. Her face was suddenly very pink. She didn't see Tom Chilton smile happily behind her back when he went up to Pollyanna's room after her.

When Doctor Chilton left, Miss Polly told Pollyanna, 'Next week you're going to a hospital. A friend of Dr Chilton's is going to care for you there. Maybe he can help

forgive (past **forgave**) to stop being angry with someone for something bad that they did

you. We're going to see. And...thank you, Pollyanna, for bringing Dr Chilton back to me – I'm very glad!'

'Oh, Aunt Polly. So you were *his* woman's hand and heart from long ago!' cried Pollyanna happily.

Some months later, a letter arrived from Pollyanna. Mrs Polly Chilton read it to her husband at breakfast:

Dear Aunt Polly and **Uncle** Tom,

Today I walked from my bed to the window. I couldn't believe it! At last I'm starting to walk!

The doctors watched and smiled when I did it. And the hospital workers had tears in their eyes. I didn't cry. I wanted to laugh and sing: I can walk! I arrived here nearly ten months ago. But I'm not worried by that. I was there at your **wedding**, after all.

It was a wonderful idea to have your wedding here – by my bed, Aunt Polly. Thank you! You always think of the gladdest things.

Soon I can go home, they say. I'd like to walk there. I don't want to take a buggy. Not when I can go on foot.

Legs are important, but you don't know it when they're working. When I lost my legs, I learnt that – and I'm very glad about it! I'm very glad about everything!

Tomorrow I'm going to walk some more – maybe to the door this time.

Lots of love to everyone,

Pollyanna

uncle the husband of your mother's sister

wedding the day when two people marry

37

READING CHECK

Match the sentence parts to tell the story in the last chapter.

a Pollyanna tells John Pendleton
b Pollyanna visits
c A car hits
d A doctor tells Aunt Polly
e John Pendleton adopts
f Aunt Polly sends Dr Chilton
g Pollyanna goes away
h Aunt Polly marries
i Pollyanna starts

1 to walk again.
2 Jimmy Bean.
3 Dr Chilton.
4 to a hospital.
5 Pollyanna.
6 about Jimmy Bean.
7 'Pollyanna's never going to walk again.'
8 Dr Chilton's rooms.
9 an invitation to visit Pollyanna.

WORD WORK

1 Correct the boxed words and write out the sentences.

a Polly's sister married a door man.
   Polly's sister married a poor man.

b My car doesn't work, can you help me to bush it?

   ....

c I felt ill so I took some medicals.

   ....

d When she heard the sad news, pears started to run down her face.

   ....

e My ankle Stan is married to my aunt Nancy.

   ....

2 **Join the word parts in the flower
(and make necessary spelling changes)
to complete the sentences.**

a Ben gave me an .....*invitation*... to his party
on Saturday.

b The .... looked at her leg but
he couldn't help her.

c I'm very angry with him and I can't
.... him.

d She hit her head badly and was
.... for two days.

e The .... was in a little old church.

for-

-ing invite un-
conscious
give special
wed

-ist -tion

GUESS WHAT

**Eleanor H. Porter wrote a book after *Pollyanna* called *Pollyanna Grows Up*.
What do you think happens in the book?**

a ☐ Pollyanna learns to walk again.

b ☐ Aunt Polly, Dr Chilton and Pollyanna visit Europe.

c ☐ Aunt Polly loses all her money.

d ☐ Pollyanna marries Jimmy Bean.

e ☐ Dr Chilton dies in a strange way.

f ☐ Pollyanna has a terrible secret.

g ☐ Pollyanna still plays the glad game.

Eleanor H. Porter

Project A *Character map*

1 Look at the 'character map' for Pollyanna. Where do these things go on it?

  a goes for walks in the woods   **c** carpets, curtains, and pictures

  b long fair hair   **d** eleven years old

Looks...

red dress
summer hat
old clothes

Is...

not afraid of things
an orphan
poor

Does...

talks a lot
plays the glad game
visits sick people
sometimes says the wrong thing
speaks to church ladies
goes to charity meetings
writes to folks out west
climbs trees

Likes...

sleeping in her aunt's bed
to help people
speaking to Nancy
new clothes
animals
people

2 **Find these pages and lines in the book. Match them with different things in Pollyanna's character map on page 40.**

a page 5, lines 9–10 .....*fair hair, red dress, summer hat*..........

b page 8, lines 3–12 ....

c page 9, lines 27–31 ....

d page 10, lines 23–27 ....

e page 14, line 20 to page 15, line 21 ....

f page 17, lines 16–17 ....

g page 20, lines 14–22 ....

h page 33, lines 8–12 ....

3 **Choose a different character from the Pollyanna story. Find lines in the story about them. Make notes about them in the table.**

Character	
Looks...	
Is...	
Does...	
Likes...	

4 **Now make a character map for your chosen person. Use your notes and the character map of Pollyanna to help you.**

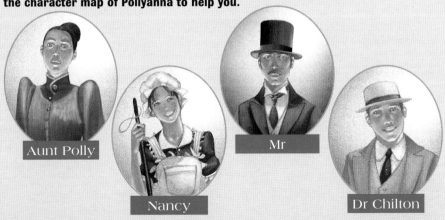

Aunt Polly

Nancy

Mr

Dr Chilton

PROJECTS

Project B · *Accident Report*

1 Read the different parts of a newspaper report about Pollyanna's accident. Put them in order: k _ _ _ _ _ _ _ _ _ _ _

a At the same time Pollyanna fell to the ground unconscious.

b **AUTOMOBILE HITS VILLAGE SCHOOLGIRL**

c He carried her home to the house of her Aunt, Miss Polly Harrington (40).

d It didn't stop, but drove away at once.

e Minutes later Mr Bell, of the Bell General Store, saw her in the street.

f Police officers are are looking for more information about the accident.

g Pollyanna started to cross the street in front of her school when she saw an automobile not far away.

h She arrived there at five o'clock, and is still in bed there unconscious today.

i She ran to the far side of the street but the automobile came at her very fast and hit her.

j They want to speak to the automobile driver, too.

k **VERMONT NEWS** November 1 1913

l Yesterday afternoon young Miss Pollyanna Whittier (11) had a bad accident as she walked home from school in Beldingsville.

2 Use the notes to complete the newspaper report about Mr John Pendleton's accident.

Accident in Pendleton Woods

Yesterday afternoon Mr .... (42) had a bad accident as he walked near .... in Pendleton Woods. He fell from .... and broke his .... After the accident Mr Pendleton ...., and he lay on the ground for ....

Then Miss Pollyanna Whittier (.........) arrived in the woods.
When she saw Mr Pendleton, she .... him. He gave her .... and she went there and .... Then she went back .... and .... to come.

Not long after that, ... (.........) arrived. He thanked Miss Whittier .... Then he took Mr Pendleton back home at once ....

Today Mr Pendleton is ...., recovering from his accident.

Accident — Pendleton Woods

John Pendleton — 42 years old
accident near big old family home
fell from some rocks
broke leg, couldn't move
lay on ground some time
girl arrived in woods for walk
Pollyanna Whittier — 11 years old
ran to help
JP gave her key to house
PW phoned for doctor
PW went back to JP, waited for help
Soon doctor arrived
Dr Tom Chilton — 40 years old
TC thanked PW for help
TC took JP home and fixed leg
Today JP at home in bed, recovering

3 **These characters from books had accidents or health problems too.**

Choose one, and write a newspaper report of his or her story. Use the grid to help you, or learn more about them on the Internet.

Character	Clara Sesemann	Colin Craven	Katy Carr
Book	Heidi	The Secret Garden	What Katy Did
Author	Johanna Spyri	Frances Hodgson Burnett	Susan Coolidge
Date	1880	1911	1872
Character's home	A big house in the city of Frankfurt in Germany	Misselthwaite Manor, a big country house in England	A house in a small town in the United States
Health problems	Clara Sesemann is the daughter of a rich family. She is paralyzed and must use a wheelchair.	A sickly boy, Colin never leaves his bed, hates the light, and feels sure he will die.	When Katy falls from a swing she hurts her back and becomes paralyzed. She stays in bed for four years.
Who helps and how?	Clara's friend Heidi invites her to her home in the Swiss mountains one summer. With mountain air, good food, and Heidi's help, Clara learns to walk.	Colin's cousin Mary Lennox takes him into a secret walled garden in a wheelchair. She helps him to take an interest in the outside world – and to walk.	Katy's invalid cousin Helen helps her to think of others. In the end, when Katy's Aunt Izzie dies, Katy learns to walk and care for her brothers and sisters.

GRAMMAR CHECK

Past Simple: Yes/No questions and short answers

We use auxiliary verbs (*did, could*) + infinitive without *to*, or was/were (main verb).

Did Nancy go to work for Miss Polly?

Was Miss Polly happy when she first met Pollyanna?

In the short answer, we reuse the auxiliary verb or was/were (main verb).

Yes, she did.

No, she wasn't. (was not)

The pronoun in the short answer matches the noun or pronoun in the question.

1 Write answers for the questions about Miss Polly. Use the short answers in the box.

Yes, she was.	~~No, she didn't.~~	Yes, she did.	No, she wasn't.	No, she couldn't.
Yes, she did.	No, she didn't.	No, she wasn't.	No, she didn't.	Yes, she could.

a Did Miss Polly have any children? No, she didn't.

b Was she beautiful when she was young? ....

c Could she go to the ladies' charity meeting? ....

d Did she love Tom Chilton? ....

e Was she a happy person at first? ....

f Did she smile when she first met Pollyanna? ....

g Could she change her heart and forgive Tom? ....

h Did she put Pollyanna in the attic at first? ....

i Did she have an accident? ....

j Was she interested in the 'glad game' at first? ....

2 Now write short answers to these questions about Pollyanna.

a Was she Miss Polly's daughter? No, she wasn't.

b Did she have a red dress? ....

c Did she live with John Pendleton? ....

d Could she help Mrs Snow to feel better? ....

e Was she sad when she met Nancy? ....

f Did she go to the charity meeting at the church? ....

g Could she walk soon after the accident? ....

GRAMMAR CHECK

Information questions and question words

We use question words in information questions.

Why does Pollyanna go to live with Miss Polly?

How much money does Miss Polly have?

What was the name of Pollyanna's mother?

We answer these questions by giving some information.

Because her mother and father are dead.

I don't know – a lot.

Jennie.

3 Complete the information questions with the question words in the box.

How	Who	How many	How long	What
When	Where	Which	Who	Why

a Q: ......Who...... likes playing the 'glad game'?

A: Pollyanna.

b Q: .... brothers does Miss Polly have?

A: She doesn't have any brothers.

c Q: .... does old Tom usually work?

A: In Miss Polly's garden.

d Q: .... does Pollyanna come to Miss Polly's home town from the west?

A: By train.

e Q: .... does it take to drive in the buggy to Miss Polly's house?

A: Not long.

f Q: .... room does Pollyanna sleep in when she first arrives?

A: The attic.

g Q: .... loved Pollyanna's mother many years ago?

A: John Pendleton.

h Q: .... does Pollyanna go to the charity meeting?

A: Because she wants to help Jimmy Bean.

i Q: .... happens to Pollyanna near the end of the story?

A: She has an accident.

j Q: .... do Aunt Polly and Dr Chilton marry?

A: After Pollyanna's accident.

GRAMMAR CHECK

Verb + infinitive or –ing form

After the verbs *begin, forget, learn, like, need, remember, want,* and *would like,* we use to + infinitive.

I'd like to read that book.

After the verbs *begin, finish, go, like, love,* and *stop* we use verb + –ing.

I love reading.

4 **Complete these sentences about the story with the *to* + infinitive or verb + –*ing* form of the verb in brackets.**

a At first, Miss Polly doesn't want `to care for` (care for) Pollyanna.

b Miss Polly begins .... (think) about her sister Jennie.

c Pollyanna loves .... (make) new friends.

d Pollyanna goes .... (look) for a new dress.

e Pollyanna wants .... (sleep) out under the night sky.

f John Pendleton stops .... (smile) because Jennie doesn't love him.

g Pollyanna likes .... (help) people with problems.

h Jimmy Bean needs .... (find) a real home and family.

i Pollyanna remembers .... (write) to the ladies at her father's church.

j John Pendleton would like .... (adopt) a child.

k Pollyanna never forgets .... (think) about poor people.

l Miss Polly likes .... (read) her niece's letter.

GRAMMAR CHECK

Prepositions

Prepositions of place tell us where something or someone is.

His father is at work today.

My niece lives by the sea.

We use prepositions too in phrases like these.

on foot (= walking)   by train/buggy/car

5 Complete the text about Pollyanna's accident with the prepositions in the box.

at	at	by	by	behind
behind	in	on	on	on

On the last day of October, Pollyanna was a) .... *at* .... school. She left and walked across the road to go home. She didn't look carefully and a car hit her. When she opened her eyes, she was b) .... home again. Nancy was there and there were some flowers c) .... the table. Dr Warren came and he put his hand d) ....
Pollyanna's head.

Later, he spoke to Miss Polly e) .... a different room. 'Between you and me, Miss Polly, I'm worried about her,' he said.

Dr Chilton went to Miss Polly's house too. Miss Polly's face was very pink and Dr Tom Chilton smiled happily f) .... her back when he went up to Pollyanna's room after her. Some months later, Miss Polly and Tom married g) .... Pollyanna's bed in hospital. Pollyanna wrote a letter to say thank you. She wanted to go home h) .... foot and not i) .... buggy. Miss Polly and Tom were happy. Pollyanna's worst days were j) .... her. Now, she could begin to play the 'glad game' again.

GRAMMAR CHECK

Past Simple: affirmative

With regular verbs we usually add –ed or –d to the infinitive without *to*.

The ladies at the charity meeting talked a lot.

Pollyanna liked talking to Jimmy Bean.

With regular verbs that end in consonant + –y, we change y into i and add –ed.

worry – Miss Polly sometimes worried about her niece.

Some verbs are irregular. You must learn their past forms.

tell – Nancy told Pollyanna about her new room.

know – Miss Polly knew John Pendleton from before.

6 **Complete the text about Pollyanna and Mrs Snow with the Past Simple form of the verbs in brackets.**

Nancy always a) ...... had ...... (have) work to do and she b) .... (can) not be with Pollyanna all the time. The little girl c) .... (be) very friendly and she d) .... (want) to know more people. One day, she e) .... (go) to visit Mrs Snow, a very sick woman. She f) .... (take) some jelly for her. The sun g) .... (come) into the room and Pollyanna h) .... (see) Mrs Snow's dark hair. That afternoon, Pollyanna i) .... (do) Mrs Snow's hair and she j) .... (put) a pink flower in it.

7 **Use the verbs in the box in the Past Simple to complete the text about Pollyanna and John Pendleton.**

find	think	~~meet~~	phone	run
	smile	walk	wear	give

On her first day at school, Pollyanna a) ...... met ...... a man in the street. He b) .... a tall black hat and a long black coat. Pollyanna c) .... at him but he didn't smile back. That night, she d) .... about the man. Why was he unhappy? One day in October, after the charity meeting, Pollyanna e) .... far into Pendleton woods. There she f) .... Mr John Pendleton on the ground. He g) .... her the key to his house. Pollyanna h) .... to the house and i) .... Dr Chilton.

GRAMMAR CHECK

Adjectives and adjective patterns

Adjectives usually go before nouns. They do not change from singular to plural.

He's a poor young man.

They're poor young men.

We can use adjective phrases after a preposition too.

Jimmy's a young boy with fair hair.

He's a thin boy in old clothes.

8 **Write complete sentences about Miss Polly with these words.**

   a Miss Polly / unhappy / woman.

      .... *Miss Polly is an unhappy woman.* .....

   b She / rich woman / big house.

      ....

   c She / angry woman / a young niece.

      ....

   d She has no dresses / nice colours on them.

      ....

   e Pollyanna sees / sad woman / a green dress.

      ....

   f Pollyanna wants to see / happy woman / friendly smile.

      ....

9 **Now write five sentences with adjectives or adjective phrases about Pollyanna.**

   a ....

   b ....

   c ....

   d ....

   e ....

GRAMMAR CHECK

Possessive adjectives

These words are possessive adjectives: my, your, his, her, its, our, and their.

We use possessive adjectives to say who someone or something belongs to.

Pollyanna arrived by train. Her dress was red. Her shoes were black.

The house was old. Its rooms were cold and empty.

10 Complete these sentences with the correct possessive adjective.

a 'I don't want to care for ...my... niece but I must do it,' said Miss Polly.

b Pollyanna looked sadly at .... room. It was small and dark.

c John Pendleton didn't smile and .... clothes were black.

d Mrs Snow looked at the flower in her hair. She loved .... colour.

e Pollyanna was sad about the church charity ladies. .... hearts were good but they did not want to adopt Jimmy.

f Pollyanna understood Jimmy. It wasn't easy for you to lose .... mother and father, she knew.

g Jimmy and Pollyanna lost .... parents when they were very young.

h Pollyanna asked her aunt, 'Can Jimmy live with us in .... house?'

i Dr Chilton saw Miss Polly with a flower in .... hair.

j '.............. legs don't work,' Pollyanna said after the accident.

DOMINOES Your Choice

Read *Dominoes* for pleasure, or to develop language skills. It's your choice.

Each *Domino* reader includes:
- a good story to enjoy
- integrated activities to develop reading skills and increase vocabulary
- task-based projects – perfect for CEFR portfolios
- contextualized grammar activities

Each *Domino* pack contains a reader, and an excitingly dramatized audio recording of the story

If you liked this *Domino*, read these:

The Wild West
John Escott

How much do you know about the Wild West? What do you know about cowboys and Indians, about wagon trails and gunfights? Inside this book you will find the true story of the Wild West, and of some of the famous people who lived and worked there. People like Wyatt Earp, Jesse James, Billy the Kid – and Annie Oakley, the best shot in the West.

Housemates
Alison Watts

Chris leaves his home in a small town in Australia to go and study at the University of Sydney. He needs to find somewhere to live. But it's not easy to find a house to share in a big city. Every house has its problems, and not all of Chris's housemates are easy to live with. In fact, some of them are very difficult people! Can Chris find the house that he needs with housemates that he can live with?

	CEFR	Cambridge Exams	IELTS	TOEFL iBT	TOEIC
Level 3	B1	PET	4.0	57–86	550
Level 2	A2–B1	KET-PET	3.0–4.0	–	390
Level 1	A1–A2	YLE Flyers/KET	3.0	–	225
Starter & Quick Starter	A1	YLE Movers	1.0–2.0	–	–